Blessings in Disguise

SpeakUp Conference

Compiled by

Living Parables of Central Florida

Blessings in Disguise

Volume 3

ISBN: 978-1-945976-53-7

Published by EA Books Publishing a division of
Living Parables of Central Florida, Inc. a 501c3
EABooksPublishing.com

Living Parables of Central Florida, a 501c3

Living Parables of Central Florida Living Parables of Central Florida, Inc., of which EABooks Publishing is a division, offers publishing contests at Christian conferences to provide opportunities for unpublished authors to be discovered and earn publishing credits. We publish high quality, self-published books that bring glory and honor to God's Kingdom.

Blessings often come disguised in hard times, difficult circumstances, broken relationships, or shattered dreams. Sometimes the blessings are unexpected hugs from God. The Bible promises us that He will turn all things for good for those who love the Lord. This is the hope believers cling to when the storm clouds gather and when the rain is so hard, we can't see the next step. May you hear the hope these stories bring and are encouraged to look for your own blessings in disguise.

ACKNOWLEDGMENTS

We'd like to thank Carol Kent and Bonnie Emmorey of the SpeakUp Conference for encouraging and equipping writers and speakers for the glory of the Kingdom of God. We wish to thank Cheri Cowell and her wonderful team at EABooks Publishing for giving us this opportunity. We thank our many friends and family for supporting us in our writing dreams. And most importantly, we want to thank our Lord and Savior Jesus Christ for His gifts—may this book bring you the honor and glory you deserve.

TABLE OF CONTENTS

Blessings in Disguise

God's Perfect Timing

Grace Tuesday

"I wish I had found you sooner so I could have loved you longer" reads a sign hanging in my house. I bought it with my husband in mind. I am ten years my husband's senior. If I had found him sooner, there may have been some legal ramifications, but the sentiment of having more time together, and loving him longer, seems so nice.

I was married once before. Shortly after graduating from college, I married my first husband. I knew before I said "I do" that marrying that man was a mistake. I was in my early twenties; naïve enough to believe the emotional abuse I suffered throughout our courtship would stop after we were married, but marriage brought physical abuse and I was living a nightmare. Despite having a post-graduate degree, I was blessed to be a stay-at-home-mom to our three children, and I was afraid if I left my abusive marriage that I would lose them. After twelve years, however, our marriage ended, and my children and I stayed together.

A year after the separation from my ex-husband, I went to lunch with a friend at a grocery store as we had done many times before. This time, however, I noticed a man dressed in an Army uniform hurrying to get some soup on his lunch break. I am not sure what came over me, but I walked over to him and struck up a conversation. After a short talk, we exchanged phone numbers and a week later we went on our first date. After that, we spent all our free time together. For the first time in over a decade, I felt happy. After so many years in a loveless marriage, having someone care for and love me the way this new man did felt gloriously foreign. He was exceptional, and my children loved him. He taught my daughter to ride a two-wheeled bicycle, and even coached one of my son's baseball teams. Within a few years we were building a new home that we could call our own. There was so much excitement in seeing our dream of a new home come to fruition. Before we moved in to the new house we decided to set a wedding date.

My ex-husband hated that I was happy with someone else. He stalked us and tried anything to come between us. He was in a new relationship too, but for some reason, he could not stay out of ours. He was causing deep rifts in the once wonderful relationships I had with my children. Despite how close my children had become with my new love, the things their father was telling them caused their relationships to deteriorate too. My heart was broken because my children believed the lies they were being told. There were countless court appearances for false allegations. I didn't see the effect the stress and trauma were taking on the beautiful relationship that my new fiancé and I were building.

A week before we were supposed to close on our new home, my faith in God was tested like it never had been before. As I did every day, I checked my email after I worked out at the gym. This time, however, my inbox was flooded with over one hundred emails from my fiancé. I thought that was strange, but I opened one. What I read didn't make sense. He said, "hi babe" and closed it with, "I love you" but I was not sure what he was referring to in the rest of the email. I opened more messages and felt more confused. I quickly realized the messages were forwarded to me from my fiancé's email, but they were originally sent to another woman. Later, I learned that my ex-husband had hacked my fiancé's email and taken pleasure in forwarding me the messages. I was crushed. Once I caught my breath and confronted him, my fiancé told me that the pressure of the court appearances and stress that my ex-husband was causing had caused him to begin the affair with this other woman as a distraction.

I did not know if we should go through with the closing of our new home or go our separate ways. But something, that today I firmly believe was God, kept telling me to stay. My ex-husband made sure my children knew about the affair, which only made the damage he was already causing to our relationships worse. I wondered what example I was teaching my children if I stayed. My fiancé was equally unsure of things, but we agreed that the only way we would get through this was if we went to couples counseling. It took many months, if not years, to feel like I could trust him again. Nothing will ever justify infidelity, but in time I understood how the kind of stress we were under could cause someone to make a poor decision. We worked hard, and with pure reliance on God we strengthened our communication skills, rebuilt trust, and fell deeper in love. This complete surrender to God formed a relationship that is now stronger than we ever dreamed possible.

The relationships with two of my children have not been repaired and that often brings a feeling of debilitating grief. God's grace, however, has turned what was broken into an amazing blessing. Three years after the affair that could have destroyed us, my fiancé and I were married. My husband is my rock that holds me up when I am grief-stricken. He and I celebrate the fact that we have been blessed by overcoming terrible odds. We keep God at the center of our marriage and rely on our faith to get through any difficult time. I didn't find him sooner like my sign says, but I will love him for the rest of my life. Sometimes it is impossible to see how terrible pain can be used as good, but when the storm subsides, God's perfect timing is beautifully revealed.

Grace is Joe's wife, a mom, educator, author, and speaker. She is awe-struck by the love of Jesus. During the most difficult time of her life, deeply leaning into our Lord was her lifeline. She strives to empower others to live life with a deeper trust and hope in God.

Bare Womb, Overflowing Heart

Rebecca Keys Gentzler

Cycle after cycle, the discarded red fluid flowed from my barren womb, signaling another futile attempt at conception. Salty tears and heaving sobs made monthly rounds as I eagerly watched my breasts and belly for signs of swelling. My body silently screamed, "You have lost again!" I began to grow bitter, detesting the sight of every pregnant woman. Questions, frustrations and resentment circled my mind like vultures waiting for a wounded creature to die. "Why her and not me? I did everything right and this is how I'm being rewarded?" The formula, A + B = C, wasn't working. You live right, obey God and God will reward you. "Where did I go wrong? What did I do to deserve this? Why is God punishing me? Why isn't God giving me the desire of my heart?"

I accepted Jesus when I was four and never strayed. I obeyed my parents and did what was expected of me. I loved working hard and didn't shy away from manual labor, helping my dad and grandfather on the farm.

Following college graduation, God opened an opportunity to do some missions work in the Philippines. From there I journeyed to Theological Seminary in Kansas City where I met Marty, who was studying for the ministry. We dated, fell in love, and married eight months later. Life was good and we were happy. After graduating from Seminary, we settled into the pastorate.

From the time I was a small girl, I dreamed of having a big family. God would bless us; after all, we did 'everything' right. Time passed but no baby bump appeared. Well-meaning friends and parishioners threw out advice like rice at a wedding, "just relax," "adopt, then *it* will happen," "stop wearing tight underwear," etc. Grrr. We were both tested. My husband was good to go, I was the one with the problems. Surgeries, medicine, calendar charts, prayers and pleas, but still, nothing.

When people asked why we didn't have children, my husband simply replied, "We can't," with the emphasis on *we*. Marty never blamed me for his disappointment either publicly or privately. I always felt loved, valued and cherished. He frequently informed me he was never sorry he married me, and I was more important to him than having children. His grace and compassion helped me find healing. Through daily Bible reading, praying and journaling, I learned God could handle my questions, doubts and anger. Because I felt like God had abandoned me, for a time, many scriptures nurtured and comforted my troubled spirit, such as "*My God, my God, why have you forsaken me? Why are you so far from saving me, so far from my cries of anguish? My God, I cry out by day, but you do not answer, by night, but I find no rest*" (Psalm 22:1,2 NIV). I learned that I can be real with my Heavenly Father. I began grasping the concept of offering up the sacrifice of praise. He is worthy to be praised and worshiped even when I didn't feel like it or know what He was up to.

One day during my regular scripture reading, Psalm 20:4 jumped off the page, "May he give you the desire of your heart and make all your plans succeed…May the LORD grant all your requests." I scribbled the word 'Baby' in the margin, claimed it and hung on for dear life.

I never did have the privilege of experiencing pregnancy. I grieved for years because there is a sense of loss of missing something precious that I couldn't get over. During this long process, we chose another route by taking in a brood of foster children that filled our home with snotty noses, complications from neglect and abuse, laughter and love. We sang them songs about Jesus, read Bible stories, prayed over them and anointed them with oil.

Eventually there were two precious children from two different homes that needed our long-term care, commitment and love through adoption. We witnessed God answering prayer after prayer as we truly labored in love for everything to fall into place as it should. Both adoptions are a testimony of miracles and divine interventions. To God be the glory for His mighty hand and outstretched arm to work in ways that looked impossible! Through those two, we now have four grandchildren. God did give me the desire of my heart, just wrapped in a different package. I am truly grateful we didn't throw in the towel with each other or with our commitment to God. Truly "… we know that in all things God works for the good of those who love him, who have been called according to his purpose." (Romans 8:28 NIV) My heart is full and overflowing.

Rebecca is a speaker and writer who is passionate about prayer and worship. She and her husband pastored thirty-two years. They have two children and four grandchildren. She is caretaker to her elderly mother with dementia.

God has called her to minister to women. She recently founded, 'Mothers Praying for Prodigals', www.prayerforprodigals.wordpress.com.

GOD HAS A PLAN FOR YOU

Deb Mueller

So often in our lives, the paths that God lays before us seem to be leading in every direction but the one we chose. Then, we look back and see how every little step along the way has been covered in His amazing love, forgiveness, compassion and purpose. Oh, but God knows our heart. He knows our needs. He is not surprised by the 'curves' in the road.

It would be hard for me to even think of a time when my plan was not to be a teacher. That's all I spoke about when growing up. That was the reason for every class I took and every grade I made in school. After my step father had a relocation for his job, I had to leave college and move back to our home state. I was no longer in-state and I could not afford the fees. Finishing college was to be delayed.

Instead of a degree, I began life with a wonderful man who loved me and has loved me for nearly 46 years. We then started a family and suddenly, I was knee deep in diapers! While I was learning to be a wife and a mother, God kept working out the next step.

Once our youngest was ready, He opened the door for me to teach at my church's preschool. Oh, how I loved and the daily time with the children. I loved planning and executing their activities. The best part . . . more hugs and sweetness around me at work just as I had at home. It worked perfectly with my children as they were able to attend the preschool/daycare for free. What a blessing! My finite mind was content but the church had a great split and I found myself without a job. Oh, but God had another plan!

Though the daycare job ended, one of the women I worked with at the daycare had gotten a job at a doctor's office. She told me of an opening in her office. I was hired. This led to 29 years of working in doctor's practices from receptionist to billing to management.

Oh, but God's lavish provision did not end there! The second practice that I worked for was a psychiatric and psychological practice. In God's perfect timing, He placed me in that practice when our son was experiencing the beginning of his psychiatric problems and planning suicide. I was able to get good sound information and direction that saved his life. Note: The doctors were used by God to save his life!

God directed me to another psychiatric and psychological practice 6 years later. I had no idea how hard the days ahead were going to be for our family! Both my son and daughter have had grave psychiatric issues. Both were hospitalized more than once.

At this new practice where I have now worked for 19 years, God provided direction, resources and encouragement to navigate the mental health system and lighten the load of their problems. We were also surrounded by other believers who prayed for us and led us back to trusting the Lord through it all. Like other illnesses, they are not cured, but they are alive and thriving.

It's funny. I always wanted to be a teacher, but more than anything, I wanted to be a good mother. God always gave me hands-on, practical experience to make it through the hard times with each of my children.

As a bonus, He gave me peace in times that would have been unbearable without Him. He also has given me 50 years of teaching in churches. I have had the joy of teaching from preschool to adults. Sharing His word is a joy to me.

I can't tell you what road He has planned for you, but I can tell you that His plan is perfect! I can't tell you it will be easy, but I can tell you that He is lavish in His love for you. He will not fail.

My maternal grandmother taught her children this verse to hold near their hearts: Romans 8:28: For we know that all things work together for good for those who love God, to them who are called according to His purpose. His Word is true!

Wife of 46 years to Don Mueller, mother of three and grandmother of three. A cherished child of my Heavenly Father. One of my greatest joys is studying His Word and sharing it with others. Currently leading the Women's Ministry in our church. My passion is to help families needing encouragement dealing with mental illness

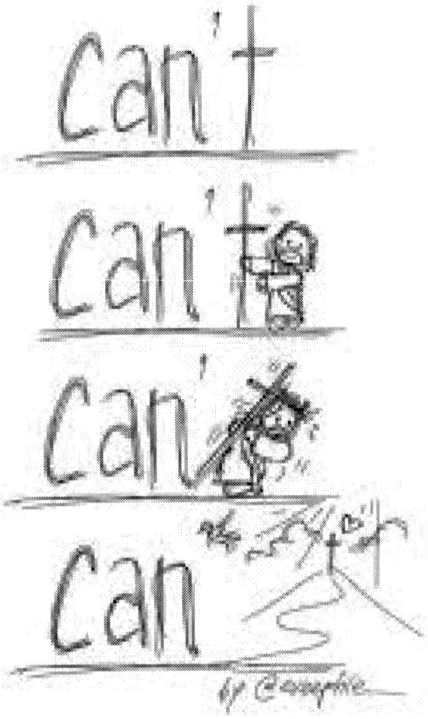
Can't
Can't
Can'
Can

Can Dad Be Fixed?

Ruth Coghill

I stared at the bare mattress on the floor. Stark. Cold. Cruel. *Why is there no furniture in Dad's room?* A scrap of paper on the window ledge caught my eye. *Is anything written on it?*

I reached deep within, fighting for strength. Now married with two little boys, I had my own life, my own challenges. *Do I need to be reminded of the early days of Dad's struggle with mental illness?* Frightful scenes from childhood flashed before me, like a movie being rewound. Those memories shocked me, making me feel like a little girl again, vulnerable and afraid.

Moments before, I had walked to the locked door and rung the buzzer. The attending nurse let me in. As soon as my feet crossed the threshold, she turned the key, preventing any escape.

White walls closed in all around. *At least this isn't like the mental hospital in Nova Scotia, its prison-like bars on the windows. This is just an ordinary hospital.*

Reluctance. Fear.

With crystal-blue eyes and silver threads running through his toffee-colored hair, Dad stood five feet eight inches tall. A crisp white shirt and polished shoes bespoke his meticulous personal care, but no belt held up his black dress pants. *Why have they taken his belt, bed frame, sheets, his personal possessions?* I dreaded the answer.

His gaze met mine, his voice weak. "This is hell! It's burning in here. See the fire marks!" *What is he pointing at?*

Straining to see, I noticed two tiny cigarette burns on the linoleum floor. *Does he really see fire burning?*

My throat tightened. I walked to the window and picked up the paper I'd seen earlier. In Dad's handwriting, barely legible, a verse from Isaiah 26:3, it read, "Thou wilt keep him in perfect peace, whose mind is stayed on thee: because he trusteth in thee."

I gritted my teeth. *What kind of peace makes a born-again Christian feel like he is in hell?* I clenched my fists, angry that my dad had taken a doctor-prescribed, addictive drug for over fifteen years without much supervision. Angry God hadn't healed him. Angry the promises of peace weren't working for him.

But by far, the strongest emotion, creeping up from the depths of my being, choking me, was... fear. Fear for today. Fear for tomorrow. Fear his medication wasn't working. Fear for my mom. *What will become of her, of him?*

Can Dad be fixed? While growing up, my three sisters and I experienced Dad as an excellent, homespun doctor. He calmly but enthusiastically dealt with our injuries. A gentle touch, a kind word, and a dab of Watkins ointment—in no time at all broken skin healed, the bandage came off, and life carried on. So simple. I longed to apply a Band-Aid to Dad now. But where do you put the Band-Aid when you can't see the wound?

Numbness crept through me. Dad trusted God with his life and often recited from Psalm 91. "He that dwelleth in the secret place of the most High shall abide under the shadow of the Almighty." *This isn't fair!* Our conversation grew awkward as the minutes dragged on. As I prepared to leave Dad questioned, "Honey, would you sing for me before you go?"

Sing for you — here in this hell?

Dad's rich tenor voice had often filled our family home with old hymns or silly little homemade rhymes.

16

What could I sing that would make my dad better? I believed in miracles. God had healed me on two occasions. My heart pounded, my thoughts spiraled. Then, with incomprehensible strength, I began to sing one of his favorites:

I'd rather have Jesus than silver or gold.
I'd rather be His than have riches untold
I'd rather have Jesus than houses or lands,
I'd rather be led by His nail-pierced hand.

Every word came through loud and clear. The composer's testimony, his desire for Jesus above all, rang into every corner, into every dark place in that psychiatric ward. Attending staff listened from a nearby nurse's station. My throat tightened as I choked out, "I'd rather have Jesus than anything . . ." Dad and Mom had given everything to follow God's call, including our beautiful home, created from the woods behind our property and built by Dad and Grandpa. Before it was finished, the house was sold and we left our homeland, beautiful Grand Manan Island, as Dad entered pastoral ministry. Everything familiar—island life, family and friends—faded into the distance as we sailed away on the ferry, waving good-bye to the many well-wishers lining the wharf.

Dad had given up more than material possessions. *Would he rather have Jesus than his mental health?* At that moment, in that place, I wondered what my response to that question would be.

As I finished singing, a tear leaked from the corner of his eye. The desire to embrace him stayed frozen inside.

"Good-bye, Dad. See you later." The nurse led me to the exit. When I glanced back over my shoulder, he was imprisoned behind the bolted barrier, a look of desperation, of helplessness, clouding his face. In a daze, I stumbled along the sterile corridor. Every step to my car brought a flashback of the last hour—so raw, so wrong.

For many years, the stigma of mental illness clung to me like a leech, plaguing me with paralyzing lies. My godly father was overtaken by the illness at forty-five and could no longer pursue his life's dream of preaching the good news of Jesus. Until his death thirty-one years later, eating, sleeping, reading, praying, memorizing Scripture, and an hour walk in the neighborhood made up his daily agenda, hampered greatly by strong medications to control his chemical imbalance.

As a little girl, I often heard Dad joyfully recite Romans 8:28 "All things work together for good to those who love God, to those who are called according to His purpose." Dad loved God. For years, I questioned God's fairness, until the moment my spiritual eyes opened. Dad was the one person whose prayers I could count on every day. Because of his illness, his schedule had been freed up to spend more time with the Lord he loved. I've been blessed with a father who passed on his love for God and His Word. And now I am the bearer of the good news.

Ruth Coghill is an international speaker, author and founder of *Words To Inspire—Lifelong Empowerment From God's Word*. This ministry exists to provide resources to strengthen each person's faith through the application of God's Word. She is currently writing four Bible studies called the WOW series and a soon to be released book *Unborn. Untold. True Stories of abortion and God's Healing Grace*. Ruth is mother of four adult children and 'nana' to thirteen grandchildren. She and her husband, Bob, reside in Kawartha Lakes, Canada.

Brothers, Baseballs & Broken Bones

Karen Wagner

Grief stormed in without warning. My prayers were a mix of "God, WHY are you allowing all of this pain?" to "God please use this for good someday, please bring growth from all of this pain"

My older brother Brian was larger than life! He stood a massive 6'8" tall and gave bear hugs that took your breath away. He lived life to the fullest and loved others with just as much energy. Friends were treated like family and because of his duty as a United State Marine, his life touched people from all over the world.

I remember his words and shaky voice so clearly when he called with the pet scan results. "Karen, I lit up like a Christmas tree". The cancer was everywhere. How could this be possible? This didn't make sense. He felt great, was as strong as an ox, lifting hundreds of pounds with his Cross-fit friends. He was newly married to his beautiful bride, Tracie. What should have been a celebratory time quickly turned into tragedy. Our family and his wife had just weeks to prepare for the inevitable.

God took Brian home on June 2nd. The hole that was left in our lives is larger than he was.

I was numb and I was exhausted. I began to endure the harsh reality that life must carry on, that I still had to function as mom and wife. Part of being a mom in June with a daughter who plays travel volleyball, is a week-long tournament called "Nationals", which happens to be held in Florida. Did I mention Brian died in Florida? I pulled up my proverbial boot straps, put my best team face on and got back on an airplane to Florida. I promised myself I would try to table the tears so I could enjoy this big event with my daughter.

In an effort to be social, I decided to hang out with the other parents, which somehow resulted in basketball in flip flops. I'm going on record that was one of the dumbest decisions of my life. I barely jumped, but I landed just right. My foot hurt so bad, I saw stars! When I returned home to Indiana, I received news of a confirmed fracture, crutches, a boot for 6 weeks, an unsuccessful recovery, then major surgery to repair one of the dumbest decisions of my life. I was stuck on the couch for months with nothing but my sadness and my ice packs.

Fast fore-ward a few weeks. My son Sam and I had gone to watch my husband's softball game, a chance to get off the couch and get some fresh air. We played catch together until his friend showed up and I took my rightful place on the bleachers. I hadn't even taken two steps when I heard Sam scream, "MOM"! All I saw was blood pouring from his mouth. He had been hit with a baseball and his front teeth were not in the right place. I was praising God for an orthodontist friend who was able to work on Sam immediately. After emergency braces, several months and a root canal, Sam's teeth were back in their proper place.

Lord, what are you doing?! How much can one girl take? God took my brother, part of my health and my son's health all in a matter of weeks. I had reached rock bottom. My heart was so heavy I could barely breathe. I began to pray for God to please makes sense of all if it.

A few months later I ran into a friend who had suddenly lost her brother. This is where God started to answer my prayers. I begged God to bring good from the pain, and he did exactly that. I knew precisely how my friend felt and understood her pain on a very personal level. I knew what not to say, I knew to just listen and let her tell me her story. All the pain and memories of my own experience provided the opportunity to walk alongside and support another person experiencing similar pain. I knew intimately how to comfort another hurting soul.

I wish more than anything it wasn't God's plan to take Brian so young, to allow personal, painful injuries and trauma to our own children, but I choose to trust his sovereignty. God never promised this life would be easy, but he did promise he would be with us every step of the way.

Grief has proven bittersweet. With grief, I feel deep sadness and I am fully aware of how short life is. However, with that same grief I am able to comfort and pray for others on a level that wouldn't be possible without fully experiencing the pain for myself.

As I cling to his sovereignty, I am waiting expectantly for God to continue using last summer for His glory.

As a Christian I've had the pleasure of walking with the Lord for over 30 years. As a Registered Dietitian and Certified Personal Trainer, I've had the pleasure of helping people reach their wellness goals for over 20 years. Watching God redeem brokenness is powerful and living in His grace is beautiful. God has recently called me into the role of Women's Ministry Director...my two worlds are merging and I couldn't be happier!

Bundle of Blessings

Tiffany Sims

Could it be that God allows his most treasured blessings to come to us disguised as burdens? In 2016, God sent me a pregnancy that was not a bundle of joy. My doctor told me, "Your baby has a zero percent chance of survival outside of the womb." She went on to say that if I carried my baby to term, I would be putting my life in jeopardy and that "eighty-five to ninety percent of people would terminate the pregnancy." I didn't want to die. I was only thirty-one and had a husband and twelve-year-old boy who needed me.

This news was like a dark storm. With each passing week, as the baby grew inside me, the storm got closer and darker. I was left with two options. I could carry my baby to term and risk dying. Or, I could terminate the pregnancy. But how could I kill my baby when abortion was against everything I believed?

I prayed daily, "Dear God, please take my baby so I don't have to go through this." Then I would have hope and pray the opposite, "Dear God, I know you can perform a miracle, just heal my baby so I don't have to go through this." Week after week, God did not induce a miscarriage or perform a miracle. He was not answering my cries or my prayers. My husband was supportive, but also just as perplexed and desperate for answers as I was. So I would seek answers from friends and family. Not one of them could give me a direct action. Not only was God ignoring me, but He wasn't letting my friends give me an answer either.

I continued to try to control the situation. In my mind, the best way to get through this storm as safely and quickly as possible was to terminate the pregnancy. The day before my scheduled termination, I was slouched down at my desk inside the grey walls of my cubicle at work. Co-workers typed diligently on their keyboards. However, all my focus from work was gone. A lump rose in my throat and my head pounded. Tears rolled down my cheeks continuously. I had never felt so empty, alone, and betrayed. My heart was broken. My grandma told me, "You'll know you've made the right decision when you're at peace." I certainly wasn't at peace. I was completely exhausted. Why wasn't God answering me?

In that very moment, God spoke to me. "Be still and know that I am GOD." (Psalm 46:10). That was my answer. "Be still" in Hebrew translates to "let drop" or "let go." God was telling me stop, let go, drop it, and take my hands off. He is in control. After all, He created this life inside me, and He would take this life in His own time and way. It was my duty to simply trust Him and let Him be God. "Trust in the Lord with all your hear and lean not on your own understanding; in all your ways submit to him, and he will make your paths straight." (NIV, Proverbs 3:5-6).

Immediately upon making the decision to carry my baby and "let go" of trying to control this situation, a physical peace swept over me. The tension eased and my body relaxed. The headache I had for weeks vanished. I no longer felt alone and betrayed. My lips turned up in a smile as I wiped away my tears. I was finally at peace. The peace that my grandma said I would have when I made the right decision. I scurried outside and called my husband. He also had an intuition that we should continue to carry our baby.

For the remainder of the pregnancy my faith increased. God was for me and all my hope was in Him. My husband and I planned for the birth of our daughter. We picked out a small white casket that was lined with a soft, silky plush interior and the same day, we also picked out a coming-home outfit speckled with pink roses. We trusted that our God was good and would carry us through any difficulties we faced, regardless of the outcome.

After months of anticipation, just three days before Christmas, our sweet baby girl Elyn Rose, was born. I immediately asked the doctor, "Does she have a heartbeat?" With a look of sadness, she reluctantly shook her head no. Our little girl was born directly into the arms of Jesus and was already healed, whole and complete. Knowing this gave me comfort.

God says in Jeremiah 1:5, "Before I formed you in the womb I knew you. Before you were born I set you apart, I appointed you as a prophet to the nations." This scripture assures me that Elyn's life was created with a unique purpose and even though she only lived inside the womb, she was very much a prophet, a precious testimony of the Lord.

I saw this pregnancy as a bundle of burdens. However, it wasn't a burden at all. It was a bundle of blessings all along. God blessed me with a situation that taught me what it means to solely trust Him through life's afflictions. God blessed me with a peace that surpassed all of my understanding. God blessed me with comfort during a time of mourning for our daughter. God blessed me with guidance when I thought I was lost. God blessed me with hope when I felt hopeless. "May the God of hope fill you with all joy and peace as your trust in him, so that you may overflow with hope by the power of the Holy Spirit." (Romans 5:13).

If we are in a constant effort to control the burdens in our life, we might miss all the blessings God has wrapped up within them. Not to mention, exhaust ourselves in the process. This constant effort to try to control trials in our life, in essence, doubts God's ability to carry us through those trials. We all face troubles that appear to be burdens. But perhaps, God is just telling you to "Be still and know that I am God."

God sent me Elyn Rose, my bundle of blessings from above.

Tiffany Sims is a stay-at-home mother, wife, women's bible study leader and writer. She firmly believes that sharing our personal testimonies can bring healing, hope and transformation to others. Her passion to encourage and enlighten women with God's truth has inspired her to create a blog at: www.brewmesomehope.com.

Summer "Stump" Burgers and Finding Rest

Cyndi Desjardins Wilkens

Summer is my favorite time of year. Lounging on my front deck in the middle of the forest in which I live, I can hear the birds chirping, see the leaves budding, and hear the frogs croaking.

One hot July day, while shifting positions in my big wicker chair, I found myself dreaming of my favorite summertime food. I had a relentless craving for a good cheeseburger.

As a quadruple amputee, a woman with no hands and feet, I slipped my legs back on as though I was slipping on a pair of slippers and proceeded into the kitchen.

Cooking is not an easy task for me. I had to relearn many tasks when I lost my hands and feet to necrotizing fasciitis — otherwise known as flesh-eating disease — in 2011, when my daughter was five years old and my son three months. Through losing my hands and feet, our family came to know Jesus.

Even when I had hands, I could make a really good cheeseburger. In fact, many people who visited us looked forward to tasting one of these scrumptious delights. I still make a mean cheeseburger, although now we call them "stump" burgers as I actually mold them with my residual arms, which medical professionals label "stumps". Originally, in an effort to re-bond with my children after months of rehabilitation, I gave these stumps the names, "Ren and Stumpy". One could say that Ren and Stumpy mold the burgers into an awkward but acceptable burger shape.

That July day, my craving drew me into the kitchen. As always our dog was right at my heels. Buddy is a 3-legged rescue who came to us at five weeks and has clung to me like Velcro ever since. We draw attention as we walk together. A woman with no hands and prosthetic legs accompanied by her 3-legged dog. I call us the amputee club. He is unaware of his disability and only protectively focused on mine.

I peered into the fridge, confirming that I had enough ground beef to start my stump burgers. I walked it over to my mixer that performs the task of stirring for me.

The voices of my children, who were running through the forest that surrounded the house, streamed in through my open kitchen window, background music as I worked.

After plopping the ground beef, I walked back over to the fridge and pulled out cheese, crumbled bacon, a container of pre-chopped onion, and my secret ingredient. Dinner time was approaching, so I moved the lever on my mixer to STIR and decided to set the table.

I opened the cupboard and placed my stumps around my unbreakable dishes, careful to pull out exactly four, and proceeded to the kitchen table.

I jumped as a large crash caught my attention. My heart sank as I surveyed the kitchen. The cast iron top of my mixer had become unhinged while stirring and fallen over onto the counter. Raw meat had splattered everywhere.

The frustrated, angry, burning feeling started in my imitation toes and crept up my body. Soon my heart was racing and my shoulders raised high in anger. My face burning hot, I looked out the window and up at the blue sky. *Why does everything I do have to be so frustrating, Lord?*

Why can't I just be able to make a cheeseburger?

I wanted to scream.

How would I clean up this mess with no hands? With no fingers to dig into the crevices it was a nearly impossible task.

I took a deep breath.

My shoulders slowly lowered back down into place as Buddy lapped up any meat he could find on the floor.

These moments happen often. Whether it is broken dishes, dropping my toothbrush and being unable to pick it up, or losing my phone in the car in that one spot between the seats that cannot be reached unless you have fingers.

It is in these moments that we can allow defeat to quickly seep in. But Psalm 46:1 tells us, "God is our refuge and strength."

Another deep breath. How I longed to get on my knees in the middle of the kitchen floor and cry out to Him. That's not very easy when you're on prosthetic legs, so I dismissed the thought and imagined myself on my knees.

Oh Lord, give me the strength. Please be my joy even in this situation.

Another breath. My husband and the children were a short shout away. But before I could call for them, I needed help from the one who settles my soul.

I called on Him.

How often do we find ourselves in situations that cause us to feel stressed and anxious? It is in those moments that we have the opportunity to make a 911 call to Him.

Psalm 18:4 affirms God hears our cries of distress. "In my distress I called to the Lord; I cried to my God for help. From his temple he heard my voice; my cry came before him, into his ears".

Frustration has become a big part of my life. The battle with it, and the enemy's whispers that I should just give up, can be energy consuming.

There are days when I fail.

But there are also days when I can celebrate the moment in which I imagine myself falling on my knees and placing it before the cross.

It is in those moments of surrender that I am able to find rest.

Jesus lovingly said, "Come to me, all you who are weary and burdened, and I will give you rest."

We all have burdens to carry. But those burdens can be made lighter when we simply take them to Jesus. How often do we forget that in every moment of loss and suffering in our lives, we can place our hands in His and allow Him to lead us?

As a quadruple amputee, I often have to rely on Jesus to be my hands and feet. Dallas Willard said, "You're a soul made by God, made for God, which means you were not made to be self-sufficient."

We don't have to be self-sufficient and alone, we have a mighty God who can give us that one desire... rest.

Cyndi Desjardins Wilkens is an author, speaker, quadruple amputee, wife, and mom. She has a heart for sharing her story with audiences in hopes that her transparency will shine a light for others facing an otherwise dark time. She thrives in Ontario, Canada.

Think on These Things

Jennifer Freeman

Finally, brothers, whatever is true, whatever is honorable, whatever is just, whatever is pure, whatever is lovely, whatever is commendable, if there is any excellence, if there is anything worthy of praise, think about these things.

Phil 4:8 (ESV)

Positive is a word I would use to describe myself. In fact, according to a popular personality test that rates 40 personal strengths, (Clifton StrenghsFinder) *Positivity* is my strongest character trait. Normally I would read a verse like Philippians 4:8 and feel somewhat proud that my mind naturally gravitates toward those kinds of things. In my mind this was a "look on the bright side" kind of verse that I could mentally skip over.

However, the demands of life have weighed me down more than usual. Positive thoughts haven't felt so natural. Lately my morning devotion routine has become an act of obedience instead of a true desire to spend time with God. Have you ever been there?

This time, opening my Bible to Philippians 4:8 sparked a twinge of irritation and shame instead of pride. It seemed to magnify a feeling of emptiness inside me.

I felt God nudge me to lean in, to embrace this verse as an action step toward Him. I felt him whisper that this verse is an invitation to a new way of thinking, one that surpasses mood, circumstances, and even personality. It has nothing to do with being positive. It has to do with being intentional.

Positive thinking is no match for the ups and downs of life, but thinking like God thinks can be.

I responded to God's invitation to "think on these things" by jotting down each of the descriptive words in Phil 4:8 and challenging myself to come up with at least one example that applies to my life. In my journal I wrote down these words: True, Honorable, Just, Pure, Lovely, Commendable, Excellent, Worthy of Praise.

The first few words were the hardest to think of examples for. It felt forced and even a bit silly. However, after a few minutes I could almost feel my mind expand to notice good things that I hadn't seen before. As I continued to fill the page, my mood shifted. I felt lighter and more joyful. My situation hadn't changed, but my heart did.

I repeat this exercise every time I sense a heaviness in my heart. It has allowed me to practice thinking in a way that honors God. Taking the time to intentionally choose my thoughts leads to an inside-out transformation every time.

If you are struggling to see beauty in your current circumstances, I invite you to see how God will open your mind as you *think on these things*. Take a moment to jot down your personal thoughts about each word below. It can be anything that comes to mind and is real for you. I have added a question you can ask yourself to get you started.

1. Whatever is TRUE: What do I know is 100% true?
2. Whatever is HONORABLE: What/Who do I think deserves honor? Why?
3. Whatever is JUST: Where am I seeing moral purity or things being handled fairly?
4. Whatever is PURE: What is authentic and undefiled?
5. Whatever is LOVELY: Where do I see obvious or hidden beauty?
6. Whatever is COMMENDABLE: Who/What deserves an accolade?

7. Whatever is EXCELLENT: What is the most outstanding thing I can think of?
8. Worthy of PRAISE: What am I in awe of?

Jennifer Freeman is a certified professional life and leadership coach. She loves helping others discover and maximize their natural gifts and talents in order to live fulfilling lives. She lives in Michigan with her husband and two children. Her perfect day involves sunshine, a quaint beach town along Lake Michigan, friends, family, and coffee.

"When you are in troubled and worried and sick at heart
And your plans are upset and your world falls apart,
Remember God's ready and waiting to share
The burden you find much too heavy to bear--
So with faith, "Let Go and Let GOD" lead your way
Into a brighter and less troubled day"

— Helen Steiner Rice

Blessings from Boot Camp

Laurie Shaffer

We were a young starry-eyed couple when we received our first full-time ministry position that moved our family from the fickle weather state of Michigan to sunshine filled Southwest Florida. What we never could have imagined though, was that God was going to use the next nineteen months, essentially, as a boot camp in our lives.

My husband Shannon and I met in the seventh grade when my family began attending the church that his father pastored. Some might call it love at first sight, as we dated throughout the next seven years, got engaged and then married just three days after my husband's 20th birthday. Although he had spent his entire life being prepared for music ministry, we had never entertained the idea of leaving our church home that both of our families attended and where our first child was doted upon. Yet, in November of 1998, we found ourselves interviewing for a full-time music pastor position at a church plant in Florida and moving 1,700 miles south just a few months later.

Living in the land of sunshine and palm trees felt like God's face smiling down on us in incredible pleasure and favor. For two months I kept asking myself, "What did we do to deserve this incredible blessing?" Then to everyone's shock, our Senior Pastor resigned and moved to another state. With his abrupt departure, the church was shaken and people began leaving. Before long, other staff members left as well, until just my husband, who was the music pastor, and the youth pastor remained. As we worked through

35

emotions of disappointment and confusion, we determined to remain fully committed to the remaining congregation. Each church service my husband faithfully led the people into praise and worship, helping us to forget the dwindling attendance, the declining offerings, and our now uncertain future.

What I had perceived as incredible favor from God, transformed into a season of immense trial that we began to call our Boot Camp Experience. It seemed that every day brought new challenges and lessons. In addition to his music pastor responsibilities, my husband took on projects like organizing indoor and outdoor volunteer teams to maintain the church building and grounds. We navigated working with the church board, and two different interim pastors. Some people advised us to leave, others genuinely thanked us for staying.

After months of guest speakers and several pastoral candidates, the church members cast their votes of approval for the current candidate just as we celebrated our one year anniversary at the church. As our new pastor settled in, we were filled with excited anticipation as the church moved forward with fresh vision and energy. We embraced the much needed changes being implemented in each area of the church, patting ourselves on the back that the Worship Arts department was strong and had sustained the church through that transitional year. So you can imagine my surprise when a few months later my husband came home with a serious look on his face and said, "I just finished a meeting with Pastor, and the church can't afford to keep us on full-time."

I remember driving down to the beach, sitting in the sand with the sun on my face, listening to the calming sound of ocean waves rolling in, watching the palm trees gently swaying in the breeze, and slowly coming to the realization that we were going to be saying goodbye to all of it. As we embraced this unexpected change, we questioned, "Did we miss God somewhere? Have we failed somehow? Was coming here a mistake? When we find a new job, will that be short term too? How is God using this for our good?"

God didn't answer all of those questions right away, but He faithfully provided for us. A position opened in our home state of Michigan at a church within an hour drive from our families, and with a sense of both gratitude and grieving we made the journey north.

As we celebrate over eighteen consecutive years of ministry at our current church home in Southeast Michigan, we know with certainty that the trials we faced in that tumultuous season were not the result of a mistake or a failure on our part, rather they were blessings in disguise that stretched our faith, strengthened our marriage, and shaped our character. Similar to the intense training that happens during boot camp, without the invaluable lessons that God packed into our short time in Florida, we would not have been properly equipped to effectively serve where we are today.

Blessings from our boot camp experience:
- We learned to lean on God and discovered He is always close when you're in crisis.
- We learned to lean on each other because extended family was an expensive long distance phone call away and social media hadn't been invented yet!
- We experienced God as Jehovah Jireh, our Provider. We did not incur financial debt and all of our needs were met despite the lack of a savings account and the unpredictability of a weekly pay check.
- We learned to be content with what we had, and now when God trusts us with abundance, we let it freely flow from our hands to missions work both local and abroad.

- We learned humility when pride led us to believe we were indispensable.

"And we know that all things work together for good to those who love God, to those who are the called according to *His* purpose" Romans 8:28 NKJV.

Laurie Shaffer lives in SE Michigan with her husband and three children. In a rare moment of quiet, you can find her curled up with a good book and a cup of tea, enjoying a game night with friends, or hiking to a waterfall with her family.

Brokenness, Meet Courage

Erika Crowl

*"'He will wipe away every tear from their eyes, and death shall be
no more, neither shall there be mourning, nor crying, nor pain
anymore, for the former things have passed away.' And he who
was seated on the throne said, 'Behold, I am making all things
new.'"* —Revelation 21: 4-5 (ESV)

This week I met Brokenness
I've heard her name before.
Thought I had sized her up
Known for her jagged-edged pieces,
she knocked at the door.
Through the safety of the peephole,
Flashed her wilted, weathered face.

Tap, Tap, Tap
A persistent *rap, rap, rap —*
I'm out here in the cold!
Can you see me?

This week I met Courage
Thought I knew her, too.
She phoned and left messages
but Doubt and Cowardice often ruled.
When Courage called this week,
and shared her comforting refrain,
I'm here if you need me
Come over for tea —
Better believe I grabbed my coat and raced to her door.

Courage, meet Brokenness.
Brokenness, Courage.
They skipped over the cordial
Courage took out her glue
Taking a cue from a crumpled up Plan—
Each shattered section she smoothed—

Ran a trembling finger over each point
Assembled a piece here
Another one there, with a prayer
I can't fix this myself!
She cried . . .
But Restoration sure can.

This poem is a reflection on the tension of finding our place in serving others in need while allowing God to do the healing. It's a situation I often face as a classroom teacher. When we watch brokenness on the reel of another's life—young or old—we may hesitate and con-template whether or not to help or enter in to the person's pain. My prayer is that the above words offer hope when we feel helpless and ultimately point to the Helper and Healer.

Erika Crowl is a writer, educator, and creator of The Firefly Project, a resource for writers. She is passionate about helping others to uncover hope and creativity. Connect with Erika on Instagram @erikacrowl or visit livereadwrite.com for teaching materials and book recommendations. Erika lives in New Jersey with her family.

It Was a Three-Legged Race

Heather Schneemann

"That leg has to come off TODAY." I was numb and in shock when I heard the doctor utter those words about my daughter's leg. I had a flashback to 20 years earlier when this beautiful little baby girl was born. She had ten fingers, ten toes, two arms, and two legs. Now we were being told that her right leg had to come off, or she would die. No brainer for this momma! But still so very hard.

It all began with a three-legged race at summer camp when our daughter, Rachel, was 12 years old. On the last day of camp, we went and picked our girls and their friends up, expecting to hear how wonderful camp was. Instead, Rachel came towards us on crutches! What happened?? The nurse came out and said, "It's almost laughable how many kids said they hurt something this week." Rachel filled in the gaps by telling us how she fell during a three-legged race and hurt her left ankle. We went home and nurse mom made sure she iced, elevated, and took Tylenol.

As the days—and then weeks—went by, Rachel still complained about her ankle hurting. She was also not engaging in life as she normally would. After numerous trips to the doctors, including a pain specialist at the Cleveland Clinic, Rachel was diagnosed with RSD/CRPS. Her foot had swollen to the size of a butternut squash, was many shades of purple and blue, was cold to the touch, and the pain was off the charts. Those who have experienced this awful disorder describe the pain as putting gasoline in your veins and lighting a match. At one point after another fall a

41

couple of months later, the pain spread throughout her body, rendering her paralyzed and hospitalized. My baby girl was experiencing pain worse than childbirth 24/7 and I could not do anything to help. The treatments vary, and do not always work: drugs, physical and occupational therapy, Ketamine-induced coma, epidural catheters, nerve stimulator, casts, and a LOT of psychological therapy that just made us mad. This was NOT in her head. No, she is not being a dramatic pre-teen. No, there was no traumatic event that triggered this. It was a three-legged race. This went on for months until a treatment finally worked at an in-patient rehabilitation center at the Cleveland Clinic. We didn't know it was only a temporary fix.

The years that followed brought Rachel in and out of remission. RSD/CRPS is brought on by any sort of injury or trauma to the body. At one point, she even went blind for 18 months after having her eyes dilated at a routine eye exam. Rachel became suicidal and developed an eating disorder. The one thing she could control in her life was what she ate! After more treatment centers to treat the anorexia, she was finally home and healed (even after she had an RSD/CRPS flare-up right before graduating from the treatment center when she fell while playing volleyball and hurt her knee). Somehow, she was able to finish 8th grade and then high school. Feeling great for the first time in a long time, Rachel was off to college. The night before classes began at Calvin College, we received a phone call from campus police saying Rachel had hurt her right ankle while jumping in a pond during a dorm initiation activity. Here we go again. I will never forget Rachel saying to me, "Mom, it's back." After more failed treatments and two years on crutches, the swelling was so bad that her skin was breaking. We were told at the Cleveland Clinic this time there was nothing they could do. Rachel developed lymphedema on top of the

RSD/CRPS and we were sent home to get treatment back in Michigan.

"That leg has to come off TODAY." That was the treatment. This amazing 20-year-old girl was about to lose a limb. What would her future look like? How was my momma's heart going to withstand this? "God, I have been trusting you through ALL of this. You love her more than I do. Thy will be done." Just before surgery, Rachel told us if this was going to happen, she was going to use it for good. She has stayed true to her word! She even came up with all sorts of jokes about being an amputee while in the hospital! She had me write on the board in her room a question for the doctor: "When will it grow back?" Her sense of humor and faith in God carried her through what could have been a very dark time. She inspired the rest of us to be strong and courageous. She even went surfing with Bethany Hamilton months after her amputation. The best part of the story? Her old boy "friend," Mark, came back into her life while she was recovering in the hospital. He had wanted to date Rachel before she left for college, but since she was just getting her life back at the time, she said no. In God's perfect timing, they were reunited and married 1.5 years later. On December 2, 2018, their daughter (my first grandchild), Kezia Jean, was born—a whopping 9.6 pounds. She is our "beauty from ashes." Her name actually means "gift from God" or "blessing after trials." Today, Rachel is pain-free and healthy. Amen and amen!

Who would have thought those seven little words would be a blessing in disguise?

Heather Schneemann lives in Toledo, Ohio with her husband of 29 years. They have three children, a son in-law, and a new granddaughter. She is the front of house manager at a performing arts center, leads a theater company, and participates at First Alliance Church where her husband is the Pastor.

Blessings
COUNT THEM ONE BY ONE

A God SO Near

Tamara Denis-Lewis

The darkness of witchcraft loomed greatly over my family's life. God had presented me with the pathway to Life and the floral beauty around me represented the new found joy I had in my heart.

I was   on my way to my part time job I passed wildflowers, and rows beautifully colored rose bushes, I paused and picked berries without a care in sight. Wells of refreshment overcame a dry and thirsty past. My confidence rose to the heavens as I lifted my voice to praise God who saw me and had rescued me.

As high as my confidence rose, it suddenly dropped as three large, ferocious barking dogs headed my way. Nothing could have been worse, as dogs had been a fear of mine since childhood. Moreover, the residue of the spiritual darkness of my past was ever present and overwhelmed me. Immediately I looked around, "Where is God?". "I was just talking to Him and singing to Him". The serene environment that enveloped me seconds ago was transformed into a dark dreary valley of death.

There was nowhere to run or hide, the dogs were coming my way. Their fangs ready to pierce my flesh, their eyes ready to laugh at my demise. I stood immobilized by my terror. My legs began to tremble and I could not breathe or think clearly. There was no one around to cry to for help! It was the picture of darkness that swallowed my life in my country of origin in Haiti.

My feeble voice rose and with my shaking finger--I pointed and screeched, "YOU GET AWAY FROM ME In JESUS NAME! " To my surprise, I heard whimpers from the large dogs as they turned to walk away, their tails between their hind legs. I scratched my head and wiped the pouring sweat from my brow. Feeling weak from the greatest battle of my early Christian walk, I realized that He was even more present during my time of hardship than my mountain top journey.

My imagination had drawn a vivid picture of my downfall, yet, I was not aware of the strength that lived inside until this encounter. God had not left me alone but was on the inside of me, greater than anyone that could have rescued me. While I have certainly experienced more in-depth battles since then, I grew that day in the assurance that when we face the deepest of tragedies, the hardships of life, and disappointments, it is easy to become unraveled, lose grasp of the power in our lives.

Many times the gift of His presence in our lives is masked in the hardships we face. When we press pass those hardships we often realize that He was the only one that could have brought us through and that He was with us all along. Through the journey of life we can often see that a bad situation can be a disguise for better days ahead.

Tamara Denis-Lewis uses her radical conversion experience to win souls. She is a freelance writer whose topics include intimacy in Christ and His body along with sexuality and its parallel to intimacy with Christ. She aims to impact people in her generation through profound research of scriptures webbed within her writing.

A New Coat

Gail Ramesh

The sun comes up in the morning and greets every woman the same, welcoming her to all the joy and blessings that God has in store for her in the day that is about to unfold for her. Unfortunately, within moments of her feet hitting the floor she has passed in front of at least one mirror and has begun to cast judgment on herself. Unneeded, unwanted, and unnecessary judgment. Women live in a world that is obsessed with weight, personal image and physical appearance. This can be seen in magazines, movies, and TV shows, basically, any place where women show up. There is rarely a conversation in which a woman refers to her weight as something positive or even remotely good. Weight is one of the things used in a woman's life to steal her joy, kill her spirit and destroy her self-esteem. Ask any woman about what she thinks about herself and her weight and you are likely to hear a very sad story unfold as you watch her heart descend into a black hole of despair over it. This is not the life that God intends for His Daughters. This daily routine and harsh personal criticism does no justice to the God who made her and calls her His own. Psalm 45:11 talks of a king being enthralled with his daughter's beauty. Women don't read that Scripture and hold it tight in their heart, reminding them that the God of this world not only calls her His Daughter, but calls her beautiful. Instead it's easier to cling to every negative thought the mirror spins around them. This negative alignment of a woman's heart gives her enemy an even stronger grip on her soul. Most women wade in a pool of shame, defeat and hopelessness when it comes to their weight, personal image and physical appearance. Yet, this is not what God desires for His girls!

The New Testament is sprinkled with words of freedom, hope and healing. Galatians 5:1 calls to a woman's heart, reminding her that God has set her free and He implores her to stand firm in that freedom. To not walk in the bondage that slavery brings, but to walk in the freedom that is hers! To know confidently, in the depth of her heart, that she is loved by God! Deeply and dearly loved in some powerful and intimate ways. When a woman is confident in this love her response will be that she will love God and her neighbors just as she loves herself. Loving herself, as hard as this can be, is the key to a woman's climb out of this mess. This is done by throwing off the old ideas, thoughts, images, and habits that have held women in bondage for years. She must stop believing the lies of the enemy that pull her down to the depths and no longer listen to those lies nor give them power in defining her. The flip side is found in Ephesians 4:22-24 which calls us to put on a new self, like putting on a new coat. It's silly to wear two coats when only one is needed. We boldly throw off the old one and put on the new one. At first the new self may feel a bit odd and uncomfortable, but with time it will feel normal, natural, and will be worn with joy and confidence. The longer we wear this new coat we start to truly believe what God says about us. We walk with more confidence because we realize not just who we are, but whose we are. We flood our minds with God's Word not as an act of duty, but as a desire to know more deeply the God that loves us and calls us beautiful! This new woman is not perfect, but she's on the right road. Along the way she will find other like-minded sisters going in the same direction. Together they'll keep each other on the road as they combat the lies and speak truth into each other's souls. They will steer each other clear of future pits and help each other climb out should they fall into one. They will love, care for and remind each other of their beauty as a daughter of God as they learn to love themselves more fully.

It may sound too good to be true, but not for God. In Genesis 50:20 Joseph is talking to his brothers who caused him much harm. They are begging for their lives knowing they should be punished for what they did to their brother. Joseph tells them that what was intended for evil God used to accomplish good. This is the hope we have in Jesus! When the enemy comes to steal, kill and destroy, our God is stronger and comes to bring life through the mess. He's not just bringing us a tolerable life, but John 10:10 says He is bringing us life to the full. We look back and think that all is lost and we are hopeless. But those are the lies of the enemy. When we allow God to enter this journey with us, we see what the enemy wants us to believe is for our demise, but God is going to use whatever we give to Him to draw us closer to Him. We cannot allow our weight, personal image and physical appearance to destroy us, but we trust God to use this as a pathway in which we are going to find more of our truest self and more of the God who adores us! We offer up to God what we hold in our hands, our weight, personal image and physical appearance and let Him fully take it from us. Then, as only God can do, as we press towards the cross with everything in us, redemption comes and He creates beauty from ashes and we experience the precious love that God holds for each of His girls.

Gail Ramesh is the founder of the Unveiled retreats that have been transforming women's lives from around the country since 2007. Gail has been called authentic, relevant, raw, passionate, spirit-filled, inspiring, and delightfully humorous. She teaches with surrender, leads by example and speaks truth and love that hits your core.

Small Packages

Lisa Saruga

They walked into the softly-lit restaurant, hand in hand. Christmas was elegantly articulated in the décor. The atmosphere was hushed, yet full of energetic anticipation. This was a place that people came to celebrate special events¬ — significant, life-changing moments in time.

Her excitement was building, but she needed to keep a cool head. She took in the sights around her. She heard the romantic music playing softly, punctuated by the rhythmic chiming of silverware and ringing of crystal water goblets as smiling people warmly wrapped themselves in the company of each other. Eating and drinking were ancillary to the sweet conversation and merriment. She smelled bread baking and soft smoke from a candle, accidentally snuffed by the breath of someone's laughter. She felt his hand on her back, gently guiding her toward a quaint table in a quiet corner that had been garnished with wintery flowers and the glow of candlelight. *I want to remember every detail of this night.* She smiled as the thought crossed her mind.

He pulled out a chair for her. As she sat, she noticed his eyes. They were beautiful; not just for their color, but because she could see a lifetime of love and happiness swimming within them. She also noticed the small gift bag that he retrieved from his jacket. It was decorated with the opulence of a Faberge' Egg. He had not wrapped this gift. This was a good sign. She was certain that the surprise inside was worthy of the commissioned packaging. She took a deep breath to calm herself.

He pushed her chair in, sat across from her and asked, "So, do you like this place?"

"Yes. It is really beautiful."

They both looked around the room. As their eyes reconnected, they both began to speak at the same time. They laughed.

"It's okay," she said. "What were you going to say?"

He blushed a bit. "We've been dating just over a year now."

"Yes?" She leaned forward a bit.

"I just want you to know that this has been the best year of my life."

"Yes?" Her voice sounded eager; maybe too eager.

He pulled the gift bag out. "I want you to know that the things that are important to you are important to me too."

"Oh, I agree! I mean, I feel the same. What is important to you is important to me too." She sounded awkward.

"I brought you this gift. I really hope you understand the significance of this."

Leaning forward she said, "Oh, I do! I mean . . . I will." Her eyes dropped to her hands as she tried not to fidget.

He handed her the elaborate gift bag. She smiled, hesitated, and then reached into the bag. She felt the small box inside and her heart began to beat more loudly. She pulled the box out with great excitement, ready to make a spectacle right here in front of all the restaurant guests. But suddenly the room seemed to grow dark and still. Realization began to percolate in her mind. She stammered, "It's . . . it's a little box of cereal?"

"Yes!" he said. "Fruitloops! It's your favorite, right? I wanted to show you that I have paid attention to all the little things that you love. It *is* your favorite, right?"

Sitting back, she said, "Well, yes. It's just . . . "

Realization then crossed his face. His eyes fell as quickly as her spirits had. "Oh no," he said, "This isn't what you were expecting, is it?"

She smiled, "It's great. Really. I am glad you know the things I like."

"I am so sorry. This is not at all what you had expected." He sat back in his seat and sighed heavily. "You know, this must be exactly what it was like the day Jesus was born."

Her eyes narrowed and she gave him a curious look. "What? What are you talking about?" Suddenly, the restaurant didn't seem nearly as romantic as it had a few moments before.

"Think about it," he said. "Everyone was expecting this king to be born. They thought he would be born in some palace, surrounded by powerful people that would be able to protect him so that he could save the world. Can you imagine what they must have thought when this king—the Messiah—was born in a stable? And his parents were like . . . nobodies!"

"Yeah," she said, connecting her disappointment with the emotions of that first Christmas morning. "They must have been pretty surprised, and . . . I don't know . . . underwhelmed?"

He laughed again. "I'm sorry you were underwhelmed with your gift."

Shaking her head (and the embarrassment from her face) she said, "No. It's okay. I shouldn't have made assumptions."

He looked thoughtful. "You know what I like about us? I like that we both love Jesus and that He is at the center of our relationship. I like that we both want to share His good news of great joy. I like that, no matter what happens with us, we both know that each other will be okay. More than okay."

She studied his face. This is what she loved most about him. "You're right," she said. "We will be just fine."

He kissed her hand. "You know what else must have been surprising about Jesus? Here is this tiny little baby, wrapped up in whatever could be found, laying in a food trough, in a barn with his teenage mom and . . . *confused* dad. And wrapped up in this tiny little package were hope, love, and a future."

Taking the cereal box from her hands, he got down on one knee. "Look closer," he said. He showed her a tiny little tab on the side of the box. When he pulled the tab, the box opened to reveal the most beautiful diamond ring she had ever seen. It wasn't large or extravagant, but it shined with the promise of *hope* and *love*. She saw her *future* reflected in its sparkle.

"Would you be willing to spend the rest of your life with me . . . and Jesus?"

She realized then that blessings could be disguised in the smallest, simplest of packages.

Lisa Saruga is a Licensed Professional Counselor, Legal and Ethical Specialist, Worship Leader, Wife, Mother, Grandmother and a Child of God. It was an actual "blessing in disguise" that led to her decision to write her first book this year. You can find more about her journey at lisasaruga.com.

Refinement by Fire: The Iron Furnace

Danielle Whalen

The desires of this world seldom lead to the satisfaction and fulfillment that we often hope will quench our restless hearts. Nor does an easy path build the intended character of our true design. Defeat comes easy when we are focused on the darkness of the night, but when our perspective is anchored in the horizon, we are reminded of the heavenly home that is to come. What if the battles of our lives are in fact the blessings which serve to purify and open our hearts to the evidence of our eternal tie with God?

I remember early on in my walk and growing faith that I was blissfully ignorant. I thought I'd bought into some type of transactional relationship with God. That if I was the dutiful daughter who did and said the right things then my heavenly father would say yes to all of my demands. In this portrait of perfection, it would somehow help me hide the pain that was lingered behind the mask I wore so well. I believed the pain of my past would immediately vanish and my troubles would soon be a faint memory. I quickly found that I was not in a position to bargain with God, and the pain grew harder and harder to mask despite my self-centered efforts.

Holding on to salvation like a contractual negotiation left me feeling angrier with myself, betrayed by God, and overwhelmed by what felt like relentless punishment because I could never seem to measure up. I came to the point in my life that I was so broken there was nothing left of myself to offer, I had truly come to the end of myself. I was stripped away of everything the world told me I was, the hopes I had for myself, and the control I'd desperately grasped. But in this bare vulnerability, my heart was getting cleansed and purified to prepare an offering in righteousness. Readying me for usefulness in Kingdom purpose as His witness, not in my own vain self-seeking desires.

Throughout the Bible there are many references to a refinement process which allows our response to trials and tribulations to develop an authentic faith. The scriptures portray God's loving hand as an iron furnace used to purify, shape, and weld us into His perfect design. As our perspectives become more Christlike, we grow a deeper understanding that the Lord does not take delight in the interim pressure of this world but that our eternal value is more about the strength of our character in and with Him than the ease of our lives. The character of our hearts preserves the salvation of our faith. Spiritual edification, pruning, or discipline grows our faith in who we are in Him, guides our perspective to be more aligned with His, and teaches us how to build a spiritual stance upon His foundation of truth and righteousness that can withstand any obstacle, any trial, or war. The world will wage war against us but the blessings found through the refinement of fire—not in its absence—are Godly strength to stand in grace, eternal peace, the ability to know and receive divine love, and unwavering joy in the Lord.

"Count it all joy, my brothers, when you meet trials of various kinds, for you know that the testing of your faith produces steadfastness. And let steadfastness have its full effect, that you may be perfect and complete, lacking in nothing." James 1:2-4 (ESV).

Danielle Whalen has fifteen years of professional experience in crisis intervention. This was developed serving as a masters level clinical social worker, Coast Guard member, and ministry leader for Celebrate Recovery. She has since been dedicated to her local community through bridging the disparities of mental health and spiritual wellness.

Opportunities in Disguise

In ancient times, a king had a boulder placed on a roadway. Then he hid himself and watched to see if anyone would remove the huge rock. Some of the king's wealthiest merchants and courtiers came by and simply walked around it. Many loudly blamed the king for not keeping the roads clear, but none did anything about getting the stone out of the way. Then a peasant came along carrying a load of vegetables. Upon reaching the boulder, the peasant laid down his burden and tried to move the stone to the side of the road. After much pushing and straining, he finally succeeded. After the peasant picked up his load of vegetables, he noticed a purse lying in the road where the boulder had been. The purse contained many gold coins and a note from the king indicating that the gold was for the person who removed the boulder from the roadway. The peasant learned what many of us never understand, every obstacle is really an opportunity in disguise.

NOTHING WASTED

Angela Mitchell

To be told in 2013 that there would be a day when I would smile or laugh again I wouldn't have believed it. To be told that one day my joy and grief would walk hand in hand and I would have no guilt for *living* . . . most doubtful. However, God promised if our family would hang on and not give up, He would write the story over our brokenness that would cause us to not only *live*, but live with joy that only comes through total surrender. Just as Jesus instructed his disciples in John 6:12-"*Gather the pieces that are left over. Let nothing be wasted,*" He promises to take the ashes of our heartbreak— that which is unrecognizable—and recreate a narrative we would have never known, where not a tear is in vain.

April 27, 2013, changed life forever and challenged everything our family believed. The death of our son, (and brother to Tyler and Hayden), Coleman, brought new depths of faith, trust and forgiveness as we faced one of life's greatest tragedies. Struggling with side effects from a prescribed medication, our 17-year old son took his life. It was a decision he would have never made, had the medicine not had adverse effects on his young brain.

Coleman had a plan. He led kids to the Lord, stayed clear of drugs, alcohol and partying. His heart was to go to Uganda and assist in Watoto Child Care Ministry, having had his life forever changed after hosting five children from the Watoto Children's Choir in our home. Yet those dreams were never fulfilled, as his precious life was cut short. In this difficult and painful tragedy, our family was faced with a decision: chasing justice from malpractice or healing through the bittersweet gift of legacy?

Through much prayer we chose the type of faith challenged by Paul in 2 Corinthians 4 and focused our effort on that which is unseen — the eternal. We determined that the life of our son would not be wasted and that the ground on which the enemy tried to destroy us would one day be the ground on which we would dance! We believed Psalm 27:13-14 that promised *"the goodness of the Lord in the land of the living"* and trusted God to show His blessings in hidden places.

One year after Coleman went to heaven, we held a run, miraculously raising the needed funds to build a home in his honor at Watoto. Three years later, we saw eight precious African daughters move into his home, handpicked by God himself, and have established ministry that honors our son, and most importantly the faithful Jesus we have held to!

In the summer of 2018, our family made our first trip to Uganda, Africa where God laid out the red carpet of blessing, and we will continue to return to complete God's assignments for us. The reunion with our Watoto daughters and seeing our son's home for the first time was everything we had asked of the Lord, and we experienced a peace we had not known since Coleman's death.

In the natural realm, supernatural peace through such tragedy makes no sense. Such is God's economy. It's backwards to most, but life to those who understand it. No, we didn't walk right into peace, but went through anger, tears and even doubting. God knew we would.

In turn, we knew His heart was breaking for this pain He never wanted us to know. As for all of us, the danger isn't in our doubting God's ways, but in the departing from Him.

Just like Thomas, we had to journey through doubt, ourselves, not just rely on the words and experiences of others, so we could then lay down our right for justice *to Him*. We made the decision to receive the promise Moses gave to the Egyptians in Exodus 14:14, *"The Lord will fight for you; you need only be still."* We trusted God to be our vindicator.

As our family walks through grief, we made the decision to stand on these declarations: He has been and is faithful; we will trust even though there will not be an answer this side of heaven; and we will live with eyes fixed on eternity. We know the day is coming when the one born in a humble manger is returning a righteous judge and will make all things right! We refuse to be a casualty of the enemy and instead chose to allow beauty to rise and new purpose be established—an invitation to all of us from Jesus in His Word.

We all face grief. It may just look different. Some grieve marriages they never wanted to end, businesses that didn't succeed, infertility, miscarriage, foreclosure, physical diagnosis, wayward children, strained family relationships and much more. Out of those ashes all of us can rise by trusting in the character of a faithful God. To know Him intimately allows us to declare: *through what we don't understand, He is still good.* This is walking the faith we possess. The only way the devil gets the final word is if we allow it. It's the hardest journey ever, but when we honor and hold to Jesus we can proclaim Micah 7:8, *"Do not gloat over me, my enemy! Though I have fallen, I WILL RISE!"*

Where the feet of Coleman will never walk . . . his legacy will live forever. I will walk with a limp and will play the game of this life wounded, but I have found the one who promises to never leave or forsake me to be faithful. I am finding beauty and blessing even in the brokenness and and have seen that God will never allow the journey, whatever it may be, to be wasted. It is the same promise for you.

61

Nothing is wasted. It is the message and heart of Angela Mitchell. ngela is Ambassador Program Advisor for Watoto, Director of Marketing with Chick-fil-A and faithfully attends and serves The Refuge Church in Kannapolis, NC. Wife, Mom, lover of friends and sunshine, Angela is a grateful daughter of The Healer.

Gift of a Feather

L. A. Lester

On this day, another 'not good news' court day
 . . . where Evil seems to prevail, shame and ruin the way to accomplish.
 . . . where impossibly bad and incredulously wrong gave birth to today's events.

A brief pause is allowed, as the inmate exits squad car in route to courthouse basement door —
 . . . a brief and rare glimpse of the Father's creation with swaying trees and passing cloud. A flitting of birds.

There — a bird is flying free, outside the courthouse
 . . . yet, within the space of inches, within the brevity of seconds
 . . . unnoticed, within swirling leaf debris at his feet, a small feather, precisely lit — clings now to the inmate's sock, as if destined to be there.

And, there it stays, through many miles and hours, and much movement later,
 . . . undetected, and not noticed — until later that very day, due to circumstances very 'impersonal,' — jail issued laundry once again atop bunk arrayed,
 . . . that 'feather on the sock,' now off his foot, below the stripes — somehow catches the inmate's eye.

Pulling the feather off the sock, while between fingertips held, thoughts to mind come, "How did that . . .?" And, "Yes . . . a sparrow's feather."

That feather now kept close to heart.
A sign that he is watched over,
that his Father's eye is on—
more than the sparrow.

A Blessing in disguise ... a gift of a feather.

L.A. Lester is an elementary school teacher, whose focus is on support of English Language Learners. She was privileged to serve as a teacher in an overseas, international school for a period of five years. Presently, the author teaches and tutors in her native state of California. Her writing passion is to tell stories of Redemption.

Faithful Flowers

Roxy Wiley

Are your daffodils blooming!? Mine are coming out more and more each day. What a treat to see their bright yellow, perky flowers open in the sunshine. Daffodils are by far my favorite flower in the spring. A number of years ago, my patient husband and I actually planted hundreds of daffodil varieties across our lawn. Each year these faithful flowers announce the hope of spring. Sometimes they endure freezing temperatures and snow. Other times they bend their heavy heads under a deluge of rain. It's a joy to pick some to adorn my kitchen island, but I leave most of them to pop color as the lawn wakes up from its long winter's nap.

Over the past year, in my role as Director of Ministry to Women, I experienced multiple struggles and relationship issues within our church family and I've found it difficult to keep joy and hope foremost in my mind and heart. I've prayed with and counseled many women as we've waited for the rough waters within the Body to settle. One morning during my Quiet Time by the windows in the living room, the Spirit began to give me encouragement as I checked on my faithful spring flowers. Could there be spiritual application in their presence? More than the familiar verse in Luke 12:27. What can I learn from the Creator as I enjoyed these beautiful yard decorations?

Have courage to break through the ground.
  Be strong and take heart, all you who hope in the LORD (Ps. 31:24).

Slow and steady – upward!
I can do all this through him who gives me strength
(Phil. 4:13).

Take your time but persevere.
The LORD himself goes before you and will be with you;
he will never leave you nor forsake you. Do not be afraid;
do not be discouraged (Deut. 31:8).

Don't let a little snow stop you.
When it snows, she has no fear for her household
(Prov. 31:21a).

Stand tall and reach for the Son.
So whether you eat or drink or whatever you do, do it all
for the glory of God (1 Cor. 10:31).

Watch rainstorms give life.
Ask the LORD for rain in the springtime; it is the LORD
who sends the thunderstorms. He gives showers of rain to
all people, and plants of the field to everyone (Zech. 10:1).

We grow best among friends.
Therefore, as God's chosen people, holy and dearly loved,
clothe yourselves with compassion, kindness, humility,
gentleness and patience. Bear with each other and forgive
one another if any of you has a grievance against
someone. Forgive as the Lord forgave you. And over all
these virtues put on love, which binds team all together in
perfect unity (Col. 3:12-14).

Bloom where you are planted.
Being confident of this, that he who began a good work in
you will carry it on to completion until the day of Christ
Jesus (Phil. 1:6).

Take a rest and recharge until next season.

The LORD replied, "My Presence will go with you, and I will give you rest" (Ex. 33:14).

All this from watching valiant daffodils brave the Spring.

I was encouraged.

Roxy Wiley lives in a barn home with a yard of spring daffodils and acres of grass. She loves flowers, children, and books. Roxy retired a second time and looks forward to traveling with her husband in their motor home.

Grateful for Fleas

Ravensbruck was known as one of the worst German concentration camps during World War II. When Corrie ten Boom and her sister Betsie found themselves imprisoned there, they were disgusted to discover that their barracks were infested with fleas.

When Corrie began to complain, Betsie insisted that they instead give thanks, quoting 1 Thessalonians 5:18, "In every thing give thanks: for this is the will of God in Christ Jesus concerning you." With some persuasion, Corrie finally joined her sister in thanking God for the fleas.

Several months later, the two sisters expressed their surprise that the camp guards had never come back to their barracks to disrupt or prevent the evening Bible studies they held for their fellow prisoners. It was then that Corrie realized that the very fleas which she had so despised had actually been a God-sent protection from the cruel guards.

Source: *The Hiding Place*, Corrie Ten Boom

In Your Presence

Karen Butterton

"You make known to me the path of life; in your presence there is fullness of joy; at your right hand are pleasures forevermore"
Psalm 16:11 (ESV)

It was a typical day, like any other day. Then, in one moment, I was completely broadsided. My dreams crashed, and reality was my nightmare. In one moment, my world was turned upside down. I was just informed that the cancer returned. But unlike any other cancer, Stage II or Stage III, it was Stage IV and it was metastatic. The cancer had moved into other parts of my body through the bloodstream. My oncologist informed me of the one treatment option and it had a five percent success rate to slow it down - not eliminate it. I was officially categorized as a palliative patient. The goal was to make me as comfortable as possible through the course of therapy. The prognosis was six months to live.

I was going to die.

This unexpected detour brought me to a complete stop. What do you do when you are facing your mortality and your life expectancy diminishes? How do you comprehend those words when your life's dreams and desires are destroyed and reality deprives you of hope?

I left the oncologist's office and when I arrived at home, no one was there. I walked into my bedroom, shut the door and fell to my knees and prayed; "It's not about the why,

God, it's never about the why. It's about what now? Lord, how do you want to get the glory from this? How do you want to use this cancer diagnosis to proclaim your good works in my life and my family? In what way will you use this death sentence to show your greatness and faithfulness to everyone I encounter?" This was my heartfelt cry. I knew that nothing could touch me unless my God allowed it.

My husband and son returned home. When my son left the room, my husband asked me what they found on the Pet CT Scan. How do you tell your husband that you might not live past six months? How do you tell your adopted son that he could possibly lose another mommy? My husband listened intently as I told him about the metastatic breast cancer. He got up from his chair, laid his hand on my shoulder and began to pray for me. He asked God for healing, and to help me through this cancer journey. He called out the names of God: Faithful and True. Together we proclaimed that we serve the God of the Living and not the God of the dead. He is with us and His resurrection power resides in us and His name is Jehovah Rapha, the God who heals. We proclaimed that He is our great and mighty God. Nothing is too hard for Him!

I started my cancer treatments and it was unlike anything I had ever experienced. After the chemotherapy infusion, I took to my bed and remained there. The side effects were horrible. I couldn't run with the "busy day" agenda of my life's priorities. There I was, flat on my back, wide awake, lying in bed for hours and days. I couldn't go anywhere because I needed to stay close to the bathroom and the bucket for nausea. It was in this instance that I was still, in complete silence, for the first time in years. I always prayed, talked to God, was involved in ministry and Bible reading, but in this unexpected detour, I had all the time in the world to listen. Listen to His voice and not mine. There were no other competing priorities to conceal His voice. No more distractions to elude me from His presence. There was just God and me.

Who would have thought that the most beautiful time in my life would be spending these intimate moments with God? I laid in bed, in solitude and peace and did not want to let Him go. The hours of joy and basking in His presence enveloped the room. The tears, the transparency, the comfort I experienced was unlike anything I encountered before. This disease was not a curse; it was a blessing in disguise. Despite the bad news, I was in the pasture of His presence.

Years ago, I remember hearing an old hymn that was sung by the congregation, "In the Garden", written by C. Austin Miles. After 20 years, I finally understood the great meaning of the words: "I come to the garden alone, while the dew is still on the roses. And the voice I hear falling on my ear, the Son of God discloses. And He walks with me and He talks with me and He tells me I am His own, And the joy we share as we tarry there, none other has ever known."[1]

No one can ever fathom or comprehend the joy God and I shared and experienced together. His voice, His words and His comfort lifted me physically, spiritually and emotionally. Today, we share great intimacy and I am aware of His presence more than the physical world I touch or see. His presence is with me.

Will you take moments out of your day to spend time with just Him? He's waiting to hear from you.

Dear Father, quiet me from all life's competing priorities so that I may hear your voice and bask in your presence. Teach me how to be still. Your presence is always with me; I just need You to help me be aware of You. Let me hear you, for I know you are speaking. I know You are here. Silence the noise, focus my thoughts and open my heart to receive

---

[1] https://library.timelesstruths.org/music/In_the_Garden/

from you. Remind me that when I spend time with You, there is fullness of joy in your presence.

Karen Butterton has been in the healthcare sector for over thirty years, turning around underperforming companies. She assisted her husband with ministering and supporting church plants, small groups, worship ministries, women's ministries, counseling and mentoring women. She currently attends "The Journey" in Orange City, Florida with her husband and son.

Living Parables of Central Florida

Living Parables of Central Florida, Inc., of which EABooks Publishing is a division, supports Christian charities providing for the needs of their communities and are encouraged to join hands and hearts with like-minded charities to better meet unmet needs in their communities. Annually the Board of Directors chooses the recipients of seed money to facilitate the beginning stages of these charitable activities.

Mission Statement

To empower start up, nonprofit organizations financially, spiritually, and with sound business knowledge to participate successfully as a responsible 501(c)3 organization that contributes to the Kingdom work of God.

Incubator Program

The goal of the Incubator Program: The Small Non-Profit Success Incubator Program, provides a solid foundation for running a successful non-profit through a year-long coaching process, eventually allowing these charities to successfully apply for grants and loans from others so they can further meet unmet needs in their communities.

Living Parables of Central Florida, a 501c3

73

Made in the
USA
Middletown, DE